I Won't Be Your
ESCAPE
GOAT

I Won't Be Your ESCAPE GOAT

David Carroll's Ho Made Social Media Blunders

David Carroll

Featuring Illustrations by Mike Salter

Fresh Ink Group
Guntersville

I Won't Be Your ESCAPE GOAT
David Carroll's HO MADE Social Media Blunders

Fresh Ink Group
An Imprint of:
The Fresh Ink Group, LLC
1021 Blount Avenue #931
Guntersville, AL 35976
Email: info@FreshInkGroup.com
FreshInkGroup.com

Edition 1.0 2023

Cover Art by Michael Salter
Cover by Stephen Geez / FIG
Book design by Amit Dey / FIG
Associate publisher Beem Weeks / FIG

Cataloging-in-Publication Recommendations:
HUM023000 HUMOR / Topic / Internet & Social Media
HUM000000 HUMOR / General
HUM019000 HUMOR / Topic / Language

Library of Congress Control Number: 2023911359

ISBN-13: 978-1-958922-28-6 Papercover
ISBN-13: 978-1-958922-29-3 Hardcover
ISBN-13: 978-1-958922-33-0 Ebooks

Dedication

David Carroll and Garry Mac in 2012

This book is dedicated to my friend Garry Mac, who passed away on Feb. 1, 2023. Garry would have been first in line to buy ten copies of this book, to finish off his Christmas shopping list. He was a great encourager, and he loved to laugh. Thanks for the smiles, G-Mac. This one's for you.

Introduction
from David Carroll:

As an avid social media user and fan, I have enjoyed collecting misspellings, misinterpretations and other mishaps, and included them in my blogs and newspaper columns. The response from readers was encouraging. One might even call it a *"title wave."*

Thankfully, many readers began sending in more examples of AutoCorrect and texting fails, poorly worded signs, and embarrassing invitations. Cindy Lowery in particular is always on the hunt for me.

This resulted in a series of columns, and the trend shows no signs of slowing down. You can blame it on voice to text, spell check blunders or many other factors.

No matter the reason, these social media mistakes are a good source of laughter. *(**And my own smart-aleck comments are added in bold parentheses, like this.**)* Your contributions are also welcome at RadioTV2020@yahoo.com.

Special thanks to Mike Salter for contributing the excellent illustrations and cover art. Mike is a graphic designer, book illustrator, portraitist, comic book/graphic novel artist/writer, and drummer living with his wife, Tam, and rescue dog, Penny, in Chattanooga, Tennessee.

I appreciate the hard work of Stephen Geez and Beem Weeks of Fresh Ink Group, and Jordan Rudzinski of WRCB.

Also much appreciation to my wife, Cindy, and my sons, Chris and Vince, for their patience and great advice. So with no further ***a dew***, I hope you enjoy this diversion. I ***whole hardly*** endorse it. And please: take it with a ***grain assault***.

Table of Contents

EDUCATION ERRORS:
Plane English

Comment on a search for a new school superintendent: "I hope they get a good one this time. The **steaks** are really high." *(I can't argue with that. Steaks are really expensive.)*

"We may have to change schools. The **principle** isn't very smart." *(It's the principal of the thing, right?)*

From a 10ᵗʰ grader's essay about her favorite memory from elementary school: "I always enjoyed **showin' tail**." *(That might explain all those visits to the principal's office.)*

Student complaint: "This teacher said he would **fell** me." *(Like a big oak tree.)*

Comment from a student who is thinking about skipping school: "It won't hurt me to miss a day. It's not like I'm ever going to be the **Valid Victorian**." *(Yeah, I think that's a safe bet.)*

Note to teacher from a student who was expecting a failing grade: "Just tell me how bad it was. Don't **sugar code** it." *(I heard they were teaching coding, but I had no idea.)*

Note to teacher from parent who complained about children spreading germs: "Y'all need to get serious about teaching proper **High Jean!**" *(I AM serious. And don't call me Jean.)*

Comment from an 11th grader who was upset about a school issue: "We need a new **super attendant!**" *(Maybe one who emphasizes spelling.)*

Parent complaint to teacher: "The instructions are too hard. Can't you write it in **plane English**?" *(You know, like the airlines do.)*

"I hated being in **speling** bees. I always felt like I would **loose**." *(And you were right.)*

Parent complaint: "I may have to take this to the **school bored**." *(Surely you can muster up a little enthusiasm.)*

Student complaint about teacher: "My English teacher gave me a failing grade. She says I need to learn more about **past tents**." *(This sounds more like a history lesson.)*

"Bad spelling is our worst **enema**." *(But with you leading the fight, we'll have a good outcome.)*

"I now realize, I **shoud of** been a teacher." *(Well, there's just one small problem with that.)*

"Sadly, the days of people using proper English **have went** away." *(Yes, it is a loosing battle.)*

"I wish summer vacation would get here soon. Us teachers need a **brake!**" *(I can't top this.)*

"Believe me, if you misspell just one word, your whole text is **urined**." *(Especially if it's THAT word.)*

"That teacher thinks my son has **80 HD**. What does that even mean?" *(Not sure, but at least he's in high definition.)*

"Why are they making us go to school tomorrow? It don't make any **since**." *(You just answered your own question.)*

Missippi's literacy program shows improvement

The Associated Press

and his late wife, Sally, put up $100 million of their own money to improve "prelitera...

Newspaper headline: "**Missippi's** literacy program shows improvement." *(Looks like they still have work to do.)*

"The news said schools was closed **in clement weather**. What does that even mean anyway?" *(Just get out there and shovel some of that clement.)*

"I'm glad the schools don't teach cursive writing. My kids have already learned too many **cursive words** from those movies we get at Red Box." *(Who taught Samuel L. Jackson all those cursive words, anyway?)*

"Why do they keep saying that bullies **pray** on smaller children? I didn't think they allowed that in school." *(Make them pray on somebody their own size!)*

"So they really **clothes** school tomorrow?" *(Yep. They shirt it down.)*

Protest sign about masks outside school board meeting: "**ARE** KIDS, **ARE** CHOICE!" *(You ARE kidding, right?)*

"They're doing another **quarterly** inspection of that bridge, and it is so annoying. Do they really have to do this **twice** a year?" *(The teacher covered this in arithmetic class, but that's when you were out with the measles, right?)*

"If anyone has a child who needs help in school, I can **tudor**, and I don't charge much." *(You get what you pay for.)*

"**Congradulations** to my **daugther**, who won the **speling** bee!" *(I guess it's in her jeans.)*

Weather forces Holmes County Spelling Bee to be moved to Tursday

Newspaper headline: "Spelling Bee to be moved to **Tursday.**" *(Well, they had no choice. Everybody got snowed in on Wendsdey.)*

BRAGGING BLUNDERS:
They Wrote Their Own Wedding Vowels

"Look at my daughter. She is the most precious little **angle**." *(Especially from the 45 degree view. From 90, not so much.)*

Posted by a teen girl commenting on her boyfriend's new fragrance: "I just love his new **colon**!" *(I really hope she was talking about the fragrance.)*

Posted by a proud military family: "My uncle is a veteran of **Dessert** Storm." *(This is actually a perfect description of the sweets buffet at the Sizzler. That, my friend, is a true dessert storm.)*

"My son had a great bowling season. They should give him either a trophy or a **plague**." *(Well, no offense, Marge, but I wouldn't wish a plague on anyone.)*

Posted by a new parent of twins: "We are so proud of our twin babies! Our son is Dennis and our daughter is **Dense**." *(Give her time, she will grow out of it.)*

"**Asbestos** I can figure, I should be able to retire soon." *(As long as you don't breathe in, you might make it.)*

"Our son is about to graduate with honors. I love seeing him **sore**!" *(Hopefully he will heal after getting his diploma.)*

"That pic you sent of the dinner you made looks so tasty. **Bone apple tea**!" *(French is the most appetizing language.)*

"My son Justin pulled off quite a **feet**. He won employee of the year." *(And what size shoes does he wear?)*

"They wrote their own wedding **vowels.**" *(That couldn't have taken very long.)*

"Your granddaughter is a real **sweatie** pie!" *(Just don't say that to her face.)*

"Did you hear the good news about Arlo? He's been **indicted** into his high school's hall of fame!" *(That's the happiest indictment news, ever.)*

"Here are some pics of my little nephew. He's **tuna half** years old." *(That's great. When he turns three, let minnow.)*

"Yay me! I just got **excepted** to nursing school!" *(I'll bet you aced the exam, accept for spelling.)*

"My son has bought a farm. He has a garage, a pool and several **achers**." *(I'm happy about his garage and pool, but I hope his achers heal up soon.)*

"I'm so excited to be going to prom with my boyfriend **Brain**." *(Okay, we get it, the guy is smart. But can he dance?)*

MEDICAL MISHAPS:
Curve Your Appetite

"I'm not sure **witch** doctor will do my surgery." *(Just choose the one with the best potion.)*

"I'm having a problem with my legs. It's my **very close** veins." *(Hilda, you're a great cashier, but this is too much information.)*

"My doctor said I have to cut back on sweets, or I will get '**die of beaties**.'" *(Those beaties are scary. Almost as bad as cooties.)*

Posted by a pregnant woman seeking advice: "I'm trying to decide between natural childbirth or a **sea sexion**." *(How far out to sea would you need to go?)*

"I remember missing a whole week of school, because I was covered up with **chicken pops**." *(That's nothing. Once I ate too many McNuggets, and they had to take me to the ER.)*

"My back's actin' up. Anybody know a good **choir-practor**?" *(Why yes, I do. He is joined by other vocalists as he manipulates your spine.)*

Comment from a woman on a diet: "I need to **curve** my appetite." *(You know, Maxine, that may be what got you into trouble in the first place.)*

"My doctor says I have **carpool** tunnel syndrome." *(It's because Debra made me sit in the middle on Tuesdays and Thursdays.)*

"Please keep Henry in your thoughts. The doctor says he has an **enlarged prostitute**." *(And I'll bet getting rid of one of those can cost a lot of money.)*

"My doctor says I must be **lactose and tolerant.**" *(Not me. I have zero tolerance for reality shows, robocalls or anyone who plays the harmonica.)*

"When I was little, my mama would give me **castro** oil." *(Did you grow up in Cuba?)*

"If he don't stop drinking, he'll end up with **psoriasis** of the liver." *(Not to mention dandruff of the heart.)*

"He just got out of the hospital, with a case of **ammonia**." *(Good. We can use that to clean the house.)*

"My sister choked on some steak. Thank goodness that man was there to use the Heimlich **Remover** on her!" *(So he removed the Heimlich AND the steak?)*

"My doctor says I need to stay **hibernated**." *(Oh, my, that could take all winter.)*

"Every woman over 40 should get a **monogram** at least once a year." *(I got mine on a set of towels.)*

"I am so forgetful lately. Reckon I might have **dimension** or something?" *(It's something, all right. Now what was your question?)*

"My doctor says I need to go on a **low-crab** diet." *(This is bad news for Red Lobster.)*

"If he don't stop drinking so much, the doctor says he may have to deal with **Sir Osis of the Liver.**" *(I'd much rather interact with Sir Loin of the Outback.)*

THE AMERICAN MELON COLLIE

"I'm kind of sad, feeling a little **melon collie** today."
(I haven't heard of that particular breed.)

"My husband fell and hurt his knee again today. He is truly accident **porn**." *(Please tell me he wasn't making a video at the time.)*

"I've had to use a lot of **disaffected** spray." *(I hear it kills germs on multiple services.)*

"I will be late for work. I have a dentist **opponent**." *(Good luck to you, I hope you win!)*

"No way am I getting that vaccine. It hasn't even been approved by the **FDIC**." *(Not to mention the FAA, the FCC, the FHA or the 4-H Club.)*

"I think I may need glasses. Can someone recommend a good obstetrician?" *(Sure, but I've heard the exam is a real eye opener.)*

Parking lot sign: "COVID testing in the rear." **(Hold on. That's not what I signed up for!)**

Due to unseen circumcise, we will be closing at 6pm Friday, Jan. 13th.

Sorry for any inconvenience, management

Sign on store window: "Due to unseen **circumcise**, we will be closing at 6 p.m." *(And I thought I had an interesting day.)*

RANDOM RANTS:
Make No Misteak

"What does it mean when they talk about the **windshield** factor?" *(They're talking about how long it takes to scrape off the ice.)*

"I don't know why people like to play **Scrabel**. I think it's a **dum** game." *(That's because the rules don't make any since.)*

"Believe me, I never take anything for **granite**." *(Nor do I, unless I can get a good price on marble.)*

Response to an opposing view: "Obviously, you are **Miss Informed**." *(And have you met my friends, Miss Leading and Miss Understood?)*

25

From a spirited online debate: "**Your** a idiot." *(Sorry, dude. You just lost this argument.)*

Comment from a woman who was tired after a long day of house cleaning: "It seems like I've been **moping** all day." *(Amen, sister. I'd be moping too.)*

A comment on storm damage: "I wish the insurance company would hurry up and **asses** the damage." *(I will leave this one for you to assess.)*

"Like Deputy Barney Fife says, we just need to **nick it in the butt**." *(Elwood, you may need a new battery for your hearing aid.)*

"It says to return these forms in a **vanilla** envelope. Where can I get one of those?" *(I'd start at Baskin Robbins.)*

A post about attending a movie: "I hardly ever go to the movies. Prices are too high at the **concussion** stand." *(And you could get hurt there, too.)*

"I just take it with a **grain assault**." *(At least it's a relatively healthy assault.)*

"Bad spellers of the world, **UNTIE**!" *(Our rallying cry.)*

"It don't make no **differents**. It's **sixty-one**, or a half dozen of the other." *(If we're talking about doughnuts, I'll take the sixty-one option.)*

"I tried to explain it to him, **plaid** and simple." *(Well, that's where you went wrong, Wanda. Plaid always clashes with your leopard spot bathrobe.)*

"With all **do** respect…" *(Due tell?)*

"I've tried to find the answer everywhere, I've been **wrecking** my brain!" *(You may want to take it to the body shop.)*

"That is just the **apitamy** of stupid." *(Well, it was until now.)*

"Make no **misteak** about it, I will not tolerate an employee who can't do his job." *(Maybe your next hire should be an editor?)*

"They should be able to figure this out, it isn't **rocket surgery**." *(Where's that rocket surgeon when you need him?)*

"I don't understand why people complain about Daylight Saving Time. It gives my flowers an extra hour of sunshine!" *(Nothing is misspelled here. But somehow this just belongs.)*

"I thought I had lost the keys, but I found them in the **Chester Drawers.**" *(You know Chester, don't you? He's Buck Nekkid's first cousin.)*

"Be careful when you buy milk. Always look at the **inspiration** date." *(I just checked, and that last jug I bought is definitely not inspired.)*

"They had better hurry, I am running out of **patients.**" *(Oh, no. Will your medical practice close?)*

"Please don't take **a fence** when I say this." *(If you do, my cows might get out.)*

"Now that his business has closed, Bob will have to find a new **lively hood**." *(If you must find a new hood, make it a lively one!)*

"Everybody gets so mad about politics. Chill, people. **Clam** down! *(They're a bunch of chowder heads.)*

"We once had to live next to a chicken **coupe**." *(Well, at least it wasn't a sedan.)*

"I thought he might recognize me from school, but he didn't even **eggnollege** me." *(I guess the yolk is on you.)*

"Her husband is from one of those northern states. I think it's Detroit." *(No, wait, maybe it's Toronto.)*

"If I ever win that Powerball lottery, I would just **dye**." *(I would suggest a lighter shade.)*

"I'll cross that **bride** when I come to it." *(Trust me, you don't want to cross THAT bride.)*

"He's in charge now, for all **intensive purposes**." *(Is that like intensive care?)*

"Nobody should be **forest** to do something against their will." *(Like Smokey Bear always said, "Only you can prevent forced fires!")*

"There's so much more I could say. I'm just scratching the **service**." *(Which branch of the military are you scratching?)*

"Aw, don't pay any attention to that story. It's just an old **wise** tale." *(At least that's what my old wife said.)*

"Our nation needs time to **heel**." *(I totally get that. I have a blister on my heel.)*

Due to the Coronavirus, the CDC says people should stay 6 feet apart from each other.

If you are feeling ill, please stay home and corn teen yourself.

-The Management

Pandemic sign: "If you are feeling ill, please stay home and **corn teen** yourself." *(At least you'll get plenty of fiber.)*

"I am **litterly** so bored." *(So go pick up some trash.)*

"Does the **stuppidity** ever end?" *(Judging from this, apparently not.)*

"I don't understand why it's taking so long to legalize **marinara**!" *(Well, Congress has to approve salsa first.)*

"I have three friends who are **band** from Twitter." *(That's great! What kind of music do they play?)*

"Remember when we used to write all of our secrets in a **dairy**?" *(Sure do. And those cows never told a soul.)*

"May the **raft of God** come down on them!" *(We tried to find Noah's Ark, but this will do.)*

DRIVERS ED:
How Much Father Is It?

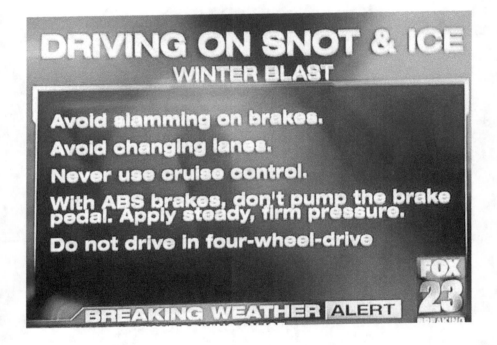

"I can't wait for spring. I don't like driving on **snot** and ice." *(I hear you. I don't like the slippery stuff either.)*

Asking for directions: "How much **father** is it 'til the interstate?" *(I'm not sure. Let me ask Father.)*

"If there's one thing I've learned about driving, you should always **air** on the side of caution." *(And if you're going to air on that side, please make sure your window is down.)*

Complaint by a man who felt he was unfairly ticketed for a traffic incident: "It was not my fault. I had the **right away**." *(At least you didn't make a getaway.)*

"He left the **seen** of the accident." *(And I scene him do it!)*

Winter weather update: "They say the main roads are clear, but the **secretary** roads are still slick." *(Note to secretaries: please work from home!)*

"That car is priced too high. I bet it cost at **lease** $30,000." *(Maybe you could just rent it for a while. Let's see, there's a name for that...)*

"I need to buy a whole new set of tires. My friend said **Michelob** is a good brand." *(I have a feeling your friend wasn't talking about tires.)*

"All these miles have really taken a **tool** on my truck." *(And if it keeps breaking down, I may take a sledgehammer to it.)*

"Herman just got a job driving a **tracker trailer.**" *(You know how he loves tracking people down.)*

Sign above busy freeway: "PLEASE DRIVE WITH **CAKE**." *(Well, okay, but I'll have to juggle that with my gravy biscuit and coffee.)*

LEGAL EAGLES:
I Won't Be Your Escape Goat

"He should deny those false allegations. If I was him, I would sue the **allegators**." *(Would that help drain the swamp?)*

"I saw it on the news. They led him away in **head cuffs**." (*Why they needed two cuffs for his head, I'll never know.*)

Comment on a suspect's mug shot: "No wonder they arrested him. He looks like a drug **attic**." (*So THAT's where he keeps them.*)

"Why are so many people getting arrested for these **Fonzie** schemes?" (*I'm not sure, but I'll bet Henry Winkler has something to do with it.*)

"If I have to, I will take him to small **clams** court!" (*Just be sure you can back up your clams.*)

"I believe my rights were **fragrantly** violated." (*Anybody with common scents can sniff that out.*)

"I won't be your **escape** goat." *(Although I am really fond of kudzu.)*

"I told the police officer the damage wasn't my fault. I hold my neighbor **reliable**." *(Like a good neighbor.)*

"I just hope this time, justice is **severed**." *(It could be, if they cut out the testimony.)*

"He didn't do nothin' wrong. It was guilt by **the sociation**." *(Then by all means, lock up the sociation.)*

"I saw the police arrest him. They took him away in **coughs**." *(It must have been allergy season.)*

"They arrested him for tax **invasion**." *(Did he break into the IRS?)*

"I need some papers signed. Is there a **noted republic** in our neighborhood?" *(Yes, his name is Dooley Noted.)*

"Surely by now the **Statue** of Limitations has run out." *(Where IS that statue, anyway?)*

"On the radio they reported heavy law enforcement **presents** on I-75." *(Santa must have come early for the police this year.)*

"They'll never take away my gun. I always have it on my **waste**." *(Yeah, I don't think your gun is going anywhere.)*

"They said I'll have to go to court if I don't bring **Affa Davis**. But I don't even know anyone by that name." *(Just go to court. Maybe Affa will show up.)*

"I was not the one who ran the red light. I should be entitled to some **condensation**!" *(Just wear this face mask with your glasses on a hot day. You'll get plenty of that.)*

"They want me to sign a **wafer**. What should I do?" *(I'd hold out for a Chips Ahoy cookie.)*

"If I have to, I'll take this all the way to the **extreme court**!" *(That reminds me. I always loved Diana Ross and the Extremes.)*

"I told them to keep my name out of this. I want to remain totally **unanimous**." *(We just voted and we were 100% anonymous.)*

"They said they were going to **dispose** the witnesses. I thought they would at least have to testify." *(Nope, they just put 'em in those big receptacles outside the courthouse.)*

"You can't believe that guy. He's a **cereal** liar." *(He'll tell you he eats a bowl of Wheaties every morning. But I know for a fact he's full of Froot Loops.)*

POLITICAL FAILS:
The Bear Necessities

"I will only vote for candidates who pledge no new **taxis**." *(We need to walk more anyway.)*

Comment on a political candidate: "I believe he will **spank** everyone's interest!" *(Be careful what you wish for.)*

Comment on a political candidate: "Well, he is definitely no **roll** model." *(However, he is an avid boater, which makes him a great row model.)*

"The president should protect our **boarders**!" *(What dangers do your boarders face? And do they pay their rent on time?)*

"The news said he's losing in the **poles**, but nobody has ever **poled** me!" *(I wouldn't complain about that. It sounds painful.)*

Comment on people with an opposing view: "They are always getting their **fillings** hurt." *(Especially if they go to the wrong dentist.)*

"That decision is bad not just for our state, but for the nation as a **hole**." *(And trust me, you don't want our nation in a hole.)*

Political comment: "That's just a load of **carp**." *(And I am nowhere near a pond.)*

"I wouldn't vote for him, he's a **trader**!" *(Cars, horses, you name it.)*

"I want someone who will drain the **swap**!" *(That's why you don't want a trader.)*

"The only reason he won is because of the electoral **collage**." *(It has taken more than 200 years to create a collage that big.)*

"If you ask me, this whole ordeal is just setting a bad **president**." *(That is not unprecedented.)*

"He is a communist **synthesizer** who should be **tired** in court." *(Maybe he's worn out from playing all that communist music.)*

"People who don't cast a **ballet** have no room to complain." *(But hopefully they can find the space to practice their jumps.)*

"He **minus** well face it. He lost the election." *(He is staying in the minus column.)*

"This nation will soon be in **dire scrapes**." *(Scratches, too?)*

"He won't answer any questions. All he ever says is, '**No comet**!'" *(Apparently he doesn't want to come clean.)*

"Our city needs to build more **infant structure**!" *(So true. There's only one McDonald's with an indoor playground.)*

"I can't believe they're considering that budget. It's all just **smoking mirrors**." *(Quick! Grab the fire distinguisher!)*

"We can't afford another government shutdown. That would be a national **apostrophe**!!" *(I see you used two explanation points.)*

"If he gets elected, I promise you gas prices will **ski rocket**." *(Especially if you live near the slopes.)*

"In my opinion, our new mayor just doesn't pass the **mustard**." *(Oh, but you should see him toss the ketchup.)*

"My vote for president doesn't count anyway. The only thing that matters is the **electrical** college." *(I guess Daddy was right. We should have gone to tech school.)*

"We need a president who can prevent a **terrace** attack!" *(And while he's at it, he needs to protect the patio and veranda too.)*

"I don't like the direction our country is headed in. Our state should just **succeed** from the union." *(Like they say, nothing secedes like secess.)*

"They're trying to **still** the election." *(Just don't let them still your heart.)*

"Why is the governor wanting money to fix our **infer-structure**? They oughta fix the roads first." *(It just seems like common cents, right?)*

"Prices are so high, we're just trying to get by with the **bear** necessities." *(We have rounded up some berries and green plants, and we're looking for a den so we can hibernate in the winter.)*

CHURCH BULLETIN
BOO-BOOS: Join Us On Sinday

"Be sure to come Sunday. We have a new **pasture**." *(I hope there's some shade.)*

"If you enjoy **sinning**, please join our choir!" *(I heard they had a record turnout that day.)*

"Join us each Sunday morning. We always offer a **worm** welcome." *(Y'all take this "fisher of men" thing seriously, don't you?)*

"At the end of the service, the ushers will visit each pew to collect your **ties**." *(But please, don't remove your shirt.)*

"Come to Vacation Bible School. We promise there will be lots of **smacks**!" *(You must know my kids pretty well.)*

"We had our largest attendance in years on **Sinday**!" *(Yes, we saw so many people who don't usually come to church.)*

"We need volunteers to help us finish **paining** the nursery." *(In fact, bring some extra pain. We don't want to run out of pain, do we?)*

"Remember that you are **butt** dust and into dust you shall return." *(For some reason, this cracks me up.)*

WANT ADS:
Ho Made Apple Butter

"I need an **English Tooter** for my son." *(Wish I could help. All I have is a Yorkshire Terrier and an Alaskan Malamute.)*

"I'd like to buy a dog, but I want her to be **spade**." *(Just make sure she shows all her cards.)*

"I need to move some dirt. Anybody got a **wheel barrel** I can borrow?" *(That almost makes sense.)*

"I need to buy a new watch. Somehow my old one got lost in the **shovel**." *(See, that's why you need a wheel barrel.)*

"I will make you a great deal on **rod iron** furniture!" *(What hath spell check wrought?)*

"We carry decorative Christmas **reefs**!" *(And you don't even have to dive into the ocean.)*

"Shop with us for a pair of lightly worn **Pat and Leather** shoes!" *(I know several folks named Pat, but have never met Leather.)*

"Wedding dress for sale. It comes with the **veal**." *(No, thanks, I'll just have the vegetables.)*

"Anybody got some **Rock-wiler** pups for sale?" *(Nope, but I can make you a deal on a Jack Daniels terrier.)*

"For sale: Like new, dining room table with all **sex** chairs included." *(Uh, I'm not sure those should go in our dining room.)*

"Missing: Orange tabby cat, neutered in the south side." *(That makes sense.)*

"Anybody want some fresh apple butter? It's all **ho made!**" *(Sure! You had me at....uh, never mind.)*

"Large dog needs a good home. Will eat anything, especially fond of children." *(Thanks for the warning.)*

SPORTS SLIP-UPS:
One for the Wrecker Books

"If you like real athletic competition, you should come to our cheerleader **trouts**." *(And be sure to stick around for the fish fry.)*

"I'm just hoping we can clinch a playoff **birth**." *(And if we do it against the Twins, that would be twice as nice.)*

"We played good 'til the end, but they won with a **buzzard** beater." *(The hard part was cleaning up all those feathers.)*

"The Knicks were down 40 points and tried to come back, but their efforts were to **Noah Vail**." *(They should have given the ball to someone else.)*

"That is definitely one for the **wrecker** books." *(In fact, it may be a new world wrecker.)*

"Alabama's defensive line will be strong this year. They have a good mix of speed, agility, and brute **forest**." *(I agree. Some of those guys are the size of redwood trees.)*

"We fans are disgusted. All the Titans do is **loose**." *(Evidently, they need to Titan up.)*

"The team don't need new players. What we need is a new **couch**!" *(In fact, just change out the whole living room suite.)*

"The Falcons could **exercise** their demons with a victory over the Saints." *(It would serve them right. Those lazy demons need a good workout.)*

"Come on out and cheer for our **baseball** team! **Kickoff** is set for 2:00 Saturday." *(I know they've been changing the rules, but this seems a little extreme.)*

"After the kids play ball, we always give them free ice cream **combs**." *(I've been wondering why their hair smells like butter pecan.)*

VACATION BLUNDERS:
Sunrise Above The Verizon

Comment about returning from vacation: "It rained the whole time, so we had to stay in our hotel **sweet**." *(Apparently, they had lots of chocolates.)*

"One time we got to see Queen Elizabeth, who was amazing. She was on the **thrown** for 70 years!" *(She had quite a rain.)*

"We had a lovely time down there! We saw so many **Anna Bellum** homes." *(Ms. Bellum was one fine architect, wasn't she?)*

Amusement park review: "My favorite ride was that real fast roller coaster. It's called The **Cannibal**." *(I truly lost my appetite.)*

"We had a great time. We went to a nightclub where me and Roscoe got to sing on the **teriyaki** machine." *(And then we had some delicious Karaoke Chicken.)*

"On the beach, we just saw a beautiful sunrise above the **Verizon**." *(I'd give it five bars.)*

"Our hotel room was **invested** with bedbugs." *(This sounds like a bad investment to me.)*

INVITATIONS TO DISASTER:
Use Our Free Ballet Parking

From a wedding invitation: "Darnell and Lola humbly request your **presents**." *(On second thought, maybe this wasn't a misspelling. Maybe they are low on silverware.)*

"If you want to come to our house, **fill free**!" *(Is there a limit on the wine glasses I can bring?)*

"If you need anything, I'm at your **disposable**." *(But you can only use me once.)*

"I have some extra tickets to the concert. If you want to go, please **massage** me." *(Can that wait until after the show?)*

From wedding party invitation: "Be sure to use our free **ballet** parking." *(I just hope the attendants are comfortable in their tutus.)*

"Please send me his funeral **arraignments**." *(I wish the law would finally leave Uncle Ned alone.)*

"For any parents who need a night off, I do baby **setting**." *(Where do you set them?)*

"You should watch this show. It is heart **worming**." *(My veterinarian would love it.)*

"We're having a meeting on **gum** violence." *(Will the rival dentist gangs be represented?)*

"I am proud to announce my engagement to Stanley. He is a wonderful **finance**." *(And after 36 monthly payments, he's all mine.)*

Christmas invitation: "Bring the kids for Breakfast with **Satan**!" *(Wow, they must have been REALLY naughty this year.)*

"Let's do some shopping. We should go **mauling**!" *(Okay, but let's get the shopping out of the way first.)*

"My son has made so much progress on the piano. I hope you can attend his **rectal**." *(Ewww. I've heard of a dinner and a show, but this is going too far.)*

"I would love to come see y'all, but I am **berried** in my work." *(So you got a job in an orchard?)*

"I've got more **collar** greens than I can eat, come get some!" *(And there's no starch!)*

"Bring your dog to our free **rabbis** clinic!" *(Well, I suppose I could. It just seems a bit unorthodox.)*

QUESTIONS, QUESTIONS:
Did You See That Obscene Jester?

"What exactly are you trying to **incinerate**?" *(Don't look at me. I don't play with fire.)*

"How will I be able to make **end's meat**?" *(Know a good butcher?)*

"Can you please be more **pacific**?" *(Only if we go out west.)*

"How many **hangers** do they have at the airport?" *(I don't know. How many coats are you bringing?)*

"I just heard that it's **musky dime** season. Does anyone know where I can find some?" *(No, but I have a drawer full of old pennies.)*

THE OBSCENE JESTER

"Did you see that obscene **jester**?" *(I remember the good old days, when jesters kept it clean.)*

"Does anyone have a good recipe I could use for **Chicken Permission**?" *(Yes, but I will have to get parmesan to give it to you.)*

"I love the new **synonym** buns at McDonald's?" *(Yes, they're just like Grammar used to make!)*

"Will adding more **installation** to my exterior walls make the house warmer?" *(Yes, but find someone who is qualified to install the installation.)*

I SAW IT ON THE TEE VEE:
Slaw News Day

"They say I can watch their news '**screaming online**.' I'm sorry, but I prefer my news without all the screaming!" *(Newscasters, please lower your voices.)*

"These TV weather people talk too much about the **Golf** of Mexico!" *(You tell 'em, Elwood. We have our own golf and it's American-made!)*

"There are too many TV commercials about **reptile** dysfunction pills." *(See you later, alligator.)*

"She surrendered to the law this morning, but the news said she is still on the **lamb**." *(If she is, she won't get very far.)*

"It must be a **slaw** news day." *(Hot dog! We could use a few of those.)*

Comment about an actress who had lost a lot of weight: "She's not just thin, she looks downright **emancipated**." *(Somewhere, Abe Lincoln is spinning in his grave.)*

Comment about celebrities' religious beliefs: "I am not a fan of Nicole Kidman. She used to be in that cult, the Church of **Cosmetology**." *(Well, that explains her nice hair.)*

"People Magazine got it right. Chris Evans truly is the **Sexist** Man Alive." *(But why are they honoring a sexist anyway, in this day and time?)*

"I saw where they just arrested five more people in a **math** lab bust." *(Something about this story doesn't add up.)*

"I really like that man on the news. He seems so **even-killed**." *(Sounds dangerous to me.)*

"That singer on American Idol is truly a **Pre-Madonna**." *(Wow, I didn't realize she was that old.)*

"They should at least give him a **constellation** prize." *(I mean, he's not asking for the sun, moon and stars.)*

FAMILY FOUL-UPS:
Wearing Hammy Downs

"I have three sisters and a **bother**." *(Yep, there's one of those in every family.)*

Facebook comment about a couple's 65th wedding anniversary: "I am impressed by their **long jevitty**." *(Especially since Elroy has such a short temper.)*

"My kids are asking for new clothes, and I tell them I always had to wear **hammy downs**." *(Sure, they smelled like bacon, but I survived.)*

"My husband is so accident **prong**." *(Whatever you do, never let him use a fork.)*

"My mom **through out** all my baseball cards." *(Yep. Right threw the window.)*

"My husband said the reason he first asked me out is because he liked my **dairy air**." *(Wait. He's comparing you with cow flatulence?)*

"When I was a kid, I loved to play **bad mitten**." *(I had one of those. There were holes in all the finger tips.)*

"I'm glad Christmas is over. At my house, I have to do all the rapping." *(I'll bet your voice could use a rest!)*

MISCELLANEOUS MISTAKES:
Bare With Me

A cheery morning greeting: "Up and **Adam**, everyone!" *(Eve could not be reached for comment.)*

"I've lived a long life. I must truly have a **garden** angel." *(Yes, Clementine, that also explains why your okra always wins the blue ribbon.)*

Sympathy note: "Elmer, my **heat** goes out to you." *(And I'm sincere about that, I'm not just spewing hot air.)*

Comment about a man who resembled the founder of KFC: "You look like **Colonial** Sanders!" *(Perhaps there is a kernel of truth here.)*

"Please **bare** with me." *(Okay, but shouldn't we at least have dinner first?)*

"I don't **mine** at all." *(Neither do I. Mining is hard work.)*

Military comment: "You can always count on the U.S. Marine **Core**." *(Sure, but don't forget the Armey and the Navey.)*

Restaurant review: "The meatloaf was okay, but I had to pour on a lot of **catch up**." *(Still, it was good to ketchup with our friends.)*

"My favorite restaurant is Chili's. Seems like they give you more bang for your **butt**." *(Well, their food can be a wee bit spicy.)*

"The man said not to send a check. He said I could use **Pay Pow**." *(Just don't shout that in public.)*

"When I walk in the woods, I can identify about 250 different **spices** of birds." *(What a sense of smell you must have.)*

"I do not tolerate **fowl** language." *(Except in the chicken house, of course.)*

"My husband ordered steak, but I had the **seizure** salad." *(I won't be making THAT mistake again!)*

"We have had some really **shirty** weather." *(Be more specific. T-shirty? Or sweat shirty?)*

"He should be in **solitaire** confinement." *(Only problem is, he's not playing with a full deck.)*

From recipe: "Be sure to use the right size **tongues** when it's time to flip the steak." *(I don't mean tiny tongues. I'm talkin' Mick Jagger-size tongues.)*

"Ask the waitress to bring the steak sauce with your meal. That will **savor** some trouble." *(And goodness knows we savor trouble.)*

"Be careful when hiking. This is peak **breading** season for snakes!" *(And if you grab one of their onion rings, they will not be happy.)*

"I can't decide between apple pie and coconut cake. Tell me, what's your favorite **desert**?" *(I've always been partial towards the Sahara, but my wife can't get enough of the Gobi.)*

"People like them are a dying **bread**." *(Yep, I'd say they're toast.)*

"Sorry for your loss. Let me offer my **symphony**." *(Well, I appreciate the offer, but I just don't have room. Maybe just the string section?)*

"Charles is the new King of England. Before ascending to the throne, he was Prince of **Whales.**" *(He can now fulfill his porpoise in life.)*

"We don't do any advertising. Our customers spread the word, so our best advertising is **mouth to mouth**." *(I'll bet "the word" isn't all they spread.)*

"You have to be careful in this **doggy dog** world." *(Tell me about it. Life is ruff.)*

"The car repair guy says I need a new **Cadillac converter**." *(I tried one of those, but it only converted my Pinto into a Maverick.)*

"That new medication I'm on has given me a new **leash** on life!" *(Except for that one weird side effect. I sure could use a good fire hydrant right now.)*

"Before y'all start yappin' about gun laws, you need to check your **fax**!" *(Yep, it could be out of paper.)*

BONUS CHAPTER 1

AUTOCORRECT ACCIDENTS:
Let Me Call You Larry

A woman was attempting to brag on her husband's memory, but she made one little texting mistake: "I can't remember that woman's name, but I'll bet Herb does. He has a **pornographic** memory!" *(Oh, so THAT's why he remembers her name.)*

A young woman texted her mother after she reunited with an old boyfriend. She intended to share the news of their engagement, but she made one mistake. "Mom, I saw John tonight. And now I'm **enraged!**" Her mother replied, "I'm not surprised, honey. I never liked him anyway!" *(Can't wait to see the wedding photos.)*

A man texted a woman friend to tell her he had just met her daughter. The word "sweet" was altered by AutoCorrect: "I finally met your daughter. Like everyone says, she is truly a **sewer** girl." *(Well, all those people can't be wrong.)*

A husband texted his wife to tell her he was busy, and would return her call later. But AutoCorrect did its magic with the word "later" and his text was sent like this: "Hey babe, let me call you **Larry**." Her response: "Well OK, but only if I can call you Curly." *(As usual, Moe, the responsible Stooge, had to straighten this out.)*

BONUS CHAPTER 2

SIGNS OF THE TIMES:
We Will Toe Your Car

Sign at restaurant entrance: "Due to high demand, we are currently out of salad **bowels**." *(We can all agree, bowels can be very demanding.)*

Sign outside church: "Don't Give in to **Satin**!" *(Absolutely. Always hold out for silk.)*

Sign outside pharmacy: "**Transfur** your prescriptions here!" *(You will appreciate our attenshun to detail!)*

Highway sign: "**Yeild** to oncoming traffic." *(The sign department had one job...)*

Sign at a customer service counter, directed at employees: "Talking Is Not **Aloud** on Cell Phones, or You Will Be **Wrote Up**!" *(So I'll just have to whisper?)*

Highway sign: "Try our **Lawn More** Repair." *(Because one lawn is never enough.)*

Fast food restaurant sign: "You may Drive **Thur**." *(But you will have to walk the other six days.)*

Sign in a doctor's office: "Warning: There are reports of a **staff** infection." *(I wouldn't want to be anywhere near that staff, would you?)*

Restaurant menu: "Try our Chicken **Flay** sandwich." *(No thanks, I'd rather have the Flay of Fish.)*

Sign in a grocery store: "Visit our candy **isle**!" *(Navigate that with care, because any spillage could call for a cleanup on Isle 7.)*

Parking lot sign: "Illegally parked cars will be **fine**."
(And dandy?)

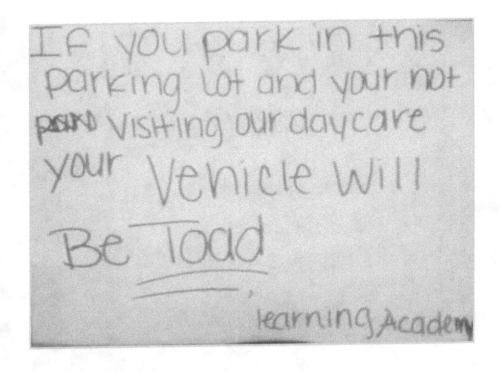

Parking lot sign: "Your vehicle will be **toad**." *(But if you kiss it, it will turn into a handsome prince.)*

Parking lot sign: "If you park here, we will **toe** your vehicle." *(And Big Earl hasn't clipped his nails since 2019, so this won't be pretty.)*

Sign on an interstate highway: "Do not cross the **medium**." *(Seriously, you don't want to get on the bad side of a fortune teller.)*

Restaurant menu item: "Try our egg **role**." *(No word on who played the egg.)*

Sign outside a retail establishment: "**Mangers** needed." *(Since this was in July, I don't think this was a Christmas season request.)*

Police department "Most Wanted" sign: "Your anonymous tip will be totally **continental**." *(And you'll get a delicious confidential breakfast, too.)*

Sign on a door inside a store: "Sorry Employees Only." ***(I guess the good employees are located in another room.)***

Sign on a school bulletin board: "Everyone is invited to the **bomb fire** 30 minutes before the game." ***(All this violence is getting out of hand.)***

Sign on doctor's office door: "Do not enter if you have **underlined** health problems." *(And if your health problems are in ALL CAPS, stay home until further notice.)*

Sign outside a fast-food restaurant: "Half-price **snakes** after 8 p.m." *(Buy two and you get a diamond back.)*

Sign outside a store window: "**Hugh** wine collection."
(But do you have any from Harold?)

Sign inside store: "We have a wine **seller** downstairs."
(By any chance, is his name Hugh?)

Restaurant sign: "Pastrami on a **beagle**." *(If it's all the same to you, I'll just have the pastrami, hold the beagle.)*

Supermarket sign: "**Boneless bananas** 69 cents a pound." *(Is that a firm price?)*

Display sign inside store: **"Banana's** 29 cents **by the each."** *(This sign does not a peel to me at all.)*

Store sign: "**Are** machine is down." **(Where do I begin?)**

Sign outside a restaurant: "Cards only, and no cash back. Sorry for the **incontinence**." *(I'm most concerned about the incontinence. Let's worry about the cards and cash later.)*

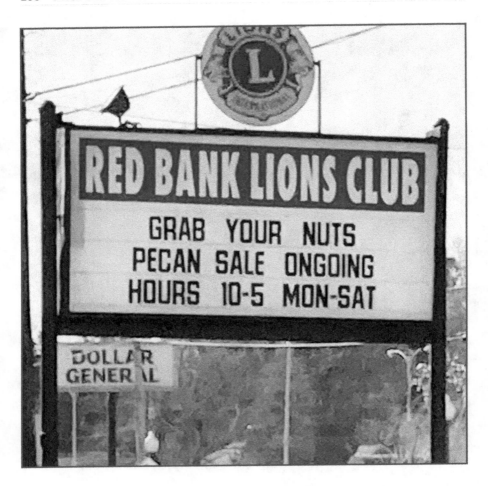

Nut sale sign: **"Grab your nuts**, pecan sale.*" (I was nut in the mood until I saw this sign.)*

Car wash sign: "**Wash and vacuum senior citizens**, $15.95." *(Hmmm…not a bad deal. Come on, Mamaw, we're goin' for a ride!)*

News anchorman: "The word should be spelled **assess**! This can't happen again."

Same guy: "**Welp!**"

Sign outside the polls: "No campaign materials or **clothing** allowed in polling place." *(Highest voter turnout ever!)*

ABOUT THE *ARTHUR*

David Carroll is a journalist in Chattanooga, Tennessee. He began his career in radio and has worked in television news since 1987. He has authored three previous books: "Chattanooga Radio and Television," "Volunteer Bama Dawg," and "Hello Chattanooga: Famous People Who Have Visited the Tennessee Valley." His weekly column appears in more than 50 newspapers. He and his wife, Cindy, have two sons, Chris and Vince. You may contact him, arrange speaking appearances or submit more social media blunders at **RadioTV2020@yahoo.com.**

Fresh Ink Group

Independent Multi-media Publisher

Fresh Ink Group / Push Pull Press

Voice of Indie / GeezWriter

Hardcovers
Softcovers
All Ebook Formats
Audiobooks
Podcasts
Worldwide Distribution

Indie Author Services
Book Development, Editing, Proofing
Graphic/Cover Design
Video/Trailer Production
Website Creation
Social Media Marketing
Writing Contests
Writers' Blogs

Authors
Editors
Artists
Experts
Professionals

FreshInkGroup.com
info@FreshInkGroup.com
Twitter: @FreshInkGroup
Facebook.com/FreshInkGroup
LinkedIn: Fresh Ink Group

Fresh Ink Group
FreshInkGroup.com

HELLO, CHATTANOOGA!

Famous People
Who Have Visited the Tennessee Valley

David Carroll

David Carroll's **Hello Chattanooga: Famous People Who Have Visited the Tennessee Valley** is a 700-page book featuring some 200 photos, more than 120 years of history and a full index allowing readers to instantly track down the date that 23-year-old Frank Sinatra made his Southern debut, President Franklin D. Roosevelt dedicated the Chickamauga Dam, or Sir Winston Churchill slammed the door of his Chattanooga hotel room in the face of a newspaper reporter.

What started as a history of Soldiers and Sailors Memorial Auditorium became much bigger, with chapters on the Tivoli Theater and all other regional venues. The book also includes all of the area's famous visitors, with many stories and photos included. Every notable politician, president, movie star, athlete, author, military figure and evangelist is listed, along with the movies and music videos that have been filmed in the Chattanooga area.

The book is published by Fresh Ink Group and personally autographed copies are available at **ChattanoogaRadioTV.com**

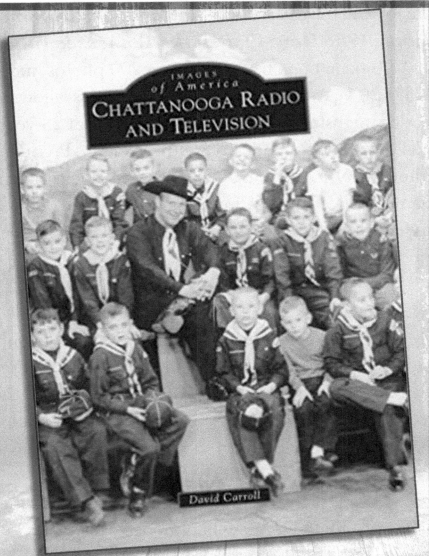

Chattanooga Radio and Television provides an informative entertaining look at Chattanooga's broadcast history through the images and stories of its participants.

Signed copies available at ChattanoogaRadioTV.com.

Printed in the USA
CPSIA information can be obtained
at www.ICGtesting.com
LVHW022101021123
762290LV00007B/15